MW01243062

Catholic Kid 365

Lent 2022

By Heath Morber

Copyright © 2022 Heath Morber
All rights reserved.

Cover design and illustration by Mary Claire Marck
(www.missmarck.com)

Sign up for the Catholic Kid 365 email list for reflections throughout the year: https://tinyurl.com/29jvmk9v

About the Author

Heath Morber is the Director of Music at Saint John's Catholic Chapel on the campus of the University of Illinois in Champaign-Urbana. There he directs two choirs and mentors Catholic university students.

Heath is the progenitor of the English Motets project (www.englishmotets.com), a co-host of the Bearded Wisdom podcast, a husband, and the father of five children. He can be reached at heath.morber@gmail.com

Note from the Author:

Kids, I'm glad you're here! The season of Lent will be a great opportunity for us to walk through salvation history, ponder the great love our Lord showed us on the cross, and put our faith into action.

How to use this book

Catholic Kid 365 is a daily resource to help kids ages 8-12 grow in their faith. We'll explore lots of things together: saints, sacraments, Bible stories, virtues, feast days and more. Everything we talk about will point us back to a God who loves us and sent his Son to redeem us.

Each day has a Bible verse about the topic, a brief entry, and then a couple steps in the "Ora et Labora" ("Pray and Work") to put the day's reflection into action. The "Deep Dive" section gives one more interesting bit of info.

You can do these daily reflections by yourself, or better yet, with your whole family. Let's have a great Lent!

Sign up for the Catholic Kid 365 email list for reflections throughout the year: https://tinyurl.com/29jvmk9v

Table of Contents

March 1—Lent

"Even now," declares the Lord, "return to me with all your heart."
(Joel 2:12)

The Church calls Lent a "joyful season." Yeesh. Giving up candy and hamburgers doesn't sound very joyful to me!

A long time ago the Church decided that the Easter feast would be so much sweeter if we spent 40 days preparing for it. The number 40 is an important one in the Bible: think of the 40 days that the rain fell on Noah and his ark, the 40 years that Moses and the Israelites spent in the desert, and the 40 days that Jesus spent fasting in the wilderness. These 40 days of Lent are a time of conversion in our lives, an opportunity to turn our hearts to the Lord and away from sin.

During this Lenten season we'll make some sacrifices to clear away anything that keeps us from loving God with all our hearts. And we'll live it with joy, preparing for that season of even greater joy: Easter.

Ora et Labora

- When you're in prayer today, ask God to reveal to you how you can remove some obstacles to your spiritual growth during this Lenten season. On Thursday we'll talk about some ideas for Lenten sacrifices.

- Lent starts tomorrow, so enjoy this Fat Tuesday!

Deep Dive

- Lent is from an Old English word that means "spring."

March 2—Ash Wednesday

All are from the dust, and to dust all return.
(Ecclesiastes 3:20)

I hope you feasted yesterday because Lent starts today!

We begin the 40 days of our Lenten journey towards Easter. If you go to Mass today, you'll get in line after the homily and receive ashes on your forehead. These ashes remind us that we come from dust and to dust we shall return, just as God told Adam.

Ashes were used as a sign of repentance throughout the Old Testament. When we walk around today and see so many other Christians with this sign on their heads, we are reminded that we are all sinners in need of God's love and mercy. Fortunately, he provides just that for us! Let's have a great Lent, kids!

Ora et Labora

- Many of our Catholic brothers and sisters only come to Mass once a year: Today! Let's pray that something they experience today at Mass will keep them coming back.

- No meat today, don't forget!

Deep Dive

- The ashes we receive on our foreheads are made from a mixture of holy water and burnt palm branches from Palm Sunday.

March 3—The Three Pillars of Lent

I turned my face to the Lord God, seeking him by prayer and pleas for mercy with fasting and sackcloth and ashes. (Daniel 9:3)

So if I'm not mistaken, during Lent the Church wants us to pray more, eat less, and give money away? Well, yes, but for a good reason.

The Church has given us three pillars to make this a fruitful Lenten season. Jesus mentioned them in the gospel yesterday: prayer, fasting, and almsgiving. We might be tempted to look at these Lenten practices as burdensome, but it's best to see these sacrifices as life-giving. Let's break them down:

Prayer: Lifting our hearts and minds to God. The relationship we build with God through prayer is what sustains us in the trials of life.

Fasting: Reducing the amount of food that we eat so we can master our appetites and not let them master us!

Almsgiving: Helping the poor by giving money and doing works of charity.

Practicing these can be challenging. But think of the opposites of our pillars of Lent: frittering our time away, eating as much as we want, and hoarding our money. We'd be lazy, chubby, and greedy! Instead, let's offer up these gifts of prayer, fasting, and almsgiving to become more like Jesus.

Ora et Labora

- We are able to fast voluntarily during Lent. But others go without food due to poverty. Let's pray for all those who struggle with hunger and food insecurity every day.

- Talk to your parents about how to incorporate these pillars into your Lenten practices.

Deep Dive

- The word roots for each of these pillars are interesting:
  Prayer: "to ask or beg"
  Fasting: "steadfast"
  Almsgiving: "giving mercy"

March 4—The Stations of the Cross

They led him away...And there followed him a great
multitude of the people and of women who were mourning
and lamenting for him.
(Luke 23:26, 27)

Kids, Lent will eventually lead us to the summit of our salvation: the Cross. We'll spend most of our Lenten Fridays focusing on Jesus's path to Calvary and what it means for us.

In the early Church, many Christians would retrace the steps of Christ's Passion in Jerusalem. This was called the *Via Dolorosa*, the "Sorrowful Way." Eventually the Church allowed Christians worldwide to imagine themselves walking the *Via Dolorosa* in their own churches and even in their homes. This devotion is called the Stations of the Cross. Most Catholic parishes have these fourteen stations throughout the body of the church building:

(1) Jesus is condemned to death.
(2) Jesus is made to bear his cross.
(3) Jesus falls the first time.
(4) Jesus meets his mother.
(5) Simon of Cyrene is made to bear the cross.
(6) Veronica wipes Jesus's face.
(7) Jesus falls the second time.
(8) The women of Jerusalem weep over Jesus.
(9) Jesus falls the third time.
(10) Jesus is stripped of his garments.
(11) Jesus is nailed to the cross.
(12) Jesus dies on the cross.
(13) Jesus is taken down from the cross.
(14) Jesus is placed in the tomb.

The Stations help us to meditate on a difficult truth: Jesus went to a painful death to give us his glorious life. Let's travel with him!

Ora et Labora

- The following dialogue happens before each cross; memorize the response and take it to heart:

  V. We adore you, O Christ, and we bless you.
  R. Because, by your holy cross, you have redeemed the world.

- Walk the Stations of the Cross on the Fridays of Lent. Many parishes have them every Friday, or you could even set up fourteen stations in your own home.

Deep Dive

- According to an ancient tradition, the Blessed Virgin Mary visited the sites of Jesus's suffering, death, and resurrection every day after his ascension into Heaven.

March 5—The Temptation of Jesus in the Desert

*For everything in the world—the lust of the flesh, the lust of
the eyes, and the pride of life—comes not from the Father,
but from the world.*
(1 John 2:16)

The Bible tells us that after Jesus had fasted for forty days, he was hungry. Yeah, I'd say so!

Before Jesus began his ministry, he went alone into the desert to fast and pray. After forty days, Satan came and tempted him three times. First, Satan told him to turn stones into bread so he could finally eat something. But Jesus didn't bite. Then he took Jesus to the top of the temple in Jerusalem and told him to throw himself off and let God send his angels to catch him. But he didn't make that leap. Finally Satan took Jesus on top of a high mountain and said all the kingdoms that he could see would be his if Jesus would only bow down and worship him. Jesus stood firm and rebuked the devil again. Jesus was preparing for his mission, and he didn't need a full stomach, flying angels, or earthly kingdoms to fulfill it. Satan left discouraged.

During our forty days in the desert of Lent, we'll be tempted, too. Those sacrifices we committed to just a few days ago will be hard to keep. But fear not! Jesus showed us the way to conquer temptation: by prayer, fasting, and keeping our eyes on our own mission to follow Jesus always.

Ora et Labora

- Temptation is something that we'll face our whole life. The St. Michael Prayer is a powerful weapon in our toolbox to overcome it.

- The Church advises us to avoid the "near occasions of sin," those situations that we can find ourselves in that tempt us to sin. Sometimes that may be being around a person that gets you into trouble, being in a place where trouble happens, or watching things on a screen that is dangerous to your soul. AVOID THOSE THINGS.

Deep Dive

- The Church teaches that temptation comes from the three enemies of the soul:
    The World: the desire for power and earthly goods.
    The Flesh: the desire for pleasures of the senses.
    The Devil: he who accuses, deceives, and plants doubts in our mind.

    All of three of these are represented in the temptation of Christ; see if you can match them up.

March 6—Covenant

"For the mountains may depart and the hills be removed, but my steadfast love shall not depart from you, and my covenant of peace shall not be removed," says the Lord.
(Isaiah 54:10)

Do you know anyone who was adopted? It's such a wonderful thing for someone to say to a child, "We want to make you a part of our family." What generous love! Or shall we say, "What covenantal love!"

There are many times in the Bible that we hear about covenants. A covenant is a promise people make to one another which binds them together into a family. Marriage is a form of covenant, as is a couple adopting a child into their family. Throughout the history of Israel, God continually reached out to mankind to adopt them into his family as his sons and daughters. Unfortunately, we also see in the Bible that mankind continually turned away from God.

In the coming days we'll see how God made covenants with Noah, Abraham, Moses, and David. But the most important covenant with mankind occurs when God sent his own son, Jesus, to bring us back into his family. We'll see how it all unfolds during this Lenten season!

Ora et Labora

- The process of adopting a child can be a long and sometimes frustrating process. Pray for couples seeking to adopt, and that all children may find themselves in a loving home.

- Ask your parents some questions about your own family history.

Deep Dive

- All of the important biblical covenants were made on hills or mountaintops. For example, God made his covenant with Noah on Mount Ararat, with Moses on Mount Sinai, and the everlasting covenant with Jesus was made on the hill of Calvary.

March 7—The Fall of Mankind

Now the serpent was more crafty than any other beast of the field that the Lord God had made.
(Genesis 3:1)

OK, the first full week of Lent is here. As we journey to the Cross and to the empty tomb, let's look backwards and see what went wrong in the first place. I'm talking about the Fall of Mankind.

We've all heard the story of Adam and Eve. We know that they were made to live together in harmony with all of God's creation in the Garden of Eden. God asked just one thing of them: do NOT eat the fruit of the Tree of the Knowledge of Good and Evil. Easy peasy, right? Wrong.

That dreaded serpent was lurking around and convinced Eve that, if they ate the fruit from that tree, they would not actually die like God said they would. Instead, they would be like God. Eve ate the fruit, so did Adam, and things went downhill from there. God was not pleased with their disobedience. He cursed the serpent and kicked Adam and Eve out of paradise. The fellowship they had with God was broken and all mankind would be separated from God until someone could repair the damage. And that someone was named Jesus.

Ora et Labora

- All the descendants of Adam and Eve—that's us—were born with the stain of Original Sin on our souls, which can only be erased through baptism. Let's pray for those who have yet to be baptized, that God may place that desire on their hearts.

- When we fall in our spiritual life, the Church calls us back to the sacrament of reconciliation. Make plans to get to confession at least once during Lent.

Deep Dive

- The Tree of the Knowledge of Good and Evil is a symbol of the boundaries that God has placed on us for our own good. Like any good parent, he gives us rules to protect us and keep us safe. Breaking those rules come with consequences.

March 8—Satan

*The great dragon was thrown down, that ancient serpent,
who is called the devil and Satan, the deceiver of the whole
world—he was thrown down to the earth, and his angels
were thrown down with him.
(Revelation 12:9)*

Remember that serpent we talked about yesterday? We saw the serpent in a different guise in last Sunday's gospel as Satan, he who tempted Christ. We also know him as the devil.

Satan was once called Lucifer, and he was one of God's angels from the dawn of creation. But he wanted more. He wanted to be equal to God. Lucifer told God, *non serviam*: I will not serve. And so, after a great battle with St. Michael and his heavenly army, Lucifer and the other rebellious angels were cast out of heaven and took up residence in hell. Satan's pride had indeed gone before his fall.

Satan and his minions still prowl around, seeking to make us stumble and stray from the right path. But we have one greater on our side, more powerful than evil, impervious to the wiles of the devil. Let's always turn to Jesus in our times of need.

Ora et Labora

- The following excerpt from 1 Peter 5:8-9 is commonly used at Night Prayer. This may be a good passage to memorize to keep us attentive: "Stay sober and alert. Your opponent the devil is prowling like a roaring lion looking for someone to devour. Resist him, solid in your faith."

- We respond to Satan's *non serviam* with our desire to serve God and one another. Do an act of service today for a family member or someone in need.

Deep Dive

- The word "Satan" is from a Greek word that means "adversary," while "Devil" is also from Greek, meaning "an accuser."

March 9—Pride and Humility

God opposes the proud, but gives grace to the humble.
(James 4:6)

Today we learn about the mother of all the sins. The one that says, "I will not serve," just like the fallen angel Lucifer said. This is the deadliest sin of them all: pride.

Pride is the love of ourselves that goes too far. It makes us think that we're smarter than our teachers, prettier than our friends, holier than the saints. We think so highly of ourselves that we have to think of others as beneath us. And the worst part of all? It's the sin that leads to all the others. It makes us say to ourselves, "Those commandments that God gave me? Nah, I can make my own decisions, thank you very much."

So how can we combat pride? By asking God for the virtue of humility. Through humility, we recognize that we are just like our fellow Christians: God's beloved sons and daughters, but sinners, too, desperately in need of the Father's mercy. Pride inflates our ego like a balloon ready to pop. Humility keeps us grounded and looking up to our loving God in wonder and obedience. One who is humble considers themself the servant of all, a fool for Christ, and strives to echo the great words of our blessed Mother: "Behold, I am the handmaid of the Lord." God, grant us humility!

Ora et Labora

- Pray that God may grant you an increase in humility during this Lenten season.

- Doing good works for others helps us to be humble servants. Do something kind for a friend, neighbor, or family member.

Deep Dive

- There is a difference in the English language between the words "proud" and "prideful." It's okay to be proud of a project you worked hard on at school, a compliment someone paid you, or a good deed you did for another person. We don't want to be prideful, however, which literally means "full of pride."

March 10—Noah

And God said, "This is the sign of the covenant I am making between me and you and every living creature with you, a covenant for all generations to come: I have set my rainbow in the clouds, and it will be the sign of the covenant between me and the earth."
(Genesis 9:12-13)

What do you think your neighbors would say if you started to make an enormous boat because God told you to? They'd probably think you were nuts. My guess is that is just what Noah's neighbors thought.

A few centuries after the creation of the world, God was not pleased with mankind. The power of sin had taken hold in the heart of man and God thought it best to just start over. A big flood should take care of it. But there was a man named Noah, a righteous man with a righteous family. God commanded him to build an enormous ark and take two of each kind of animal on it. Noah knew he would be a laughingstock in the eyes of his neighbors, but he trusted God and carried on. And sure enough, when he was done, he loaded up the ark with his family and the animals and the rain started to come. And it rained for 40 days and 40 nights, flooding the whole earth.

When the rain let up and Noah's family was finally able to stand on dry land, Noah set up an altar, offered a sacrifice to God, and made a covenant with the Lord. Noah's family was now in God's family. Since Noah trusted God, God promised never again to flood the earth, and made a rainbow as a sign of their covenant together.

Ora et Labora

- The story of Noah and the ark is a good reminder to us of how God loves the animals that he has made. Show a little extra love to your pets (if you have any) today, and let's pray for animals throughout the world that are mistreated and killed needlessly.

- With Spring around the corner, consider ways to care for the animals in your neighborhood. A few ideas if you have a yard: Setting up a bird feeder, planting a butterfly bush, or planting pollinator plants for bees.

Deep Dive

- The early Church connected Noah's ark to baptism, starting with the apostle Peter: "In (the ark) only a few people, eight in all, were saved through water. And this water symbolizes the baptism that now saves you also." (1 Peter 3:20-21)

March 11—Stabat Mater

Near the cross of Jesus stood his mother, his mother's sister, Mary the wife of Clopas, and Mary Magdalene. When Jesus saw his mother there, and the disciple whom he loved standing nearby, he said to her, "Woman, here is your son," and to the disciple, "Here is your mother."
(John 19:25-27)

Kids, Fridays in Lent are the time for us to look closely at the cross. Today we'll get a little glimpse of the love of a mother for her son.

You may remember that nearly all of Jesus's disciples ran away when the soldiers came to arrest him in the garden of Gethsemane. There was only John to stand at the foot of the Cross with Mary and just a few other faithful women. One of Jesus's final words was to entrust his mother to the care of John, who took her into his home.

The *Stabat Mater* is a beautiful Latin hymn written 600 years ago that conveys the great anguish that the Virgin Mary felt as she stood beneath the cross of Christ. It has 20 verses! It's often used during the Stations of the Cross, one verse for each station. The first verse of a well-known translation is this:

> At the cross her station keeping,
> Stood the mournful Mother weeping,
> Close to Jesus to the last.

This hymn helps us see the Crucifixion through the eyes of Mary. Let's continue to journey with her to the cross this Lenten season.

Ora et Labora

- Let's pray for sick and suffering children worldwide and the parents that care for them.

- There is a very simple, beautiful melody for the *Stabat Mater* that is familiar to most English-speaking Catholics. Learn it as a family and, if you're doing the Stations of the Cross on Fridays, incorporate it into each station. (The full hymn is easily found online. A recording can be found here: https://www.youtube.com/watch?v=eZrmnsce0vE)

Deep Dive

- The *Stabat Mater* has a very interesting rhyme scheme: AAB CCB. When you sing or say the text, notice how the last line of each stanza rhymes with the last line of the next stanza.

March 12—The Transfiguration of the Lord

A voice from heaven said, "This is my beloved Son, with whom I am well pleased."
(Matthew 3:17)

Imagine this, kids: your favorite superhero unexpectedly comes over for dinner and hangs out with you and your family. As soon as they leave, your parents say, "Don't tell ANYONE about this." Whaaat? Well, this is basically what happened to Peter, James, and John on Mt. Tabor.

Jesus had taken them up to the top of the mountain with him. The disciples were feeling a bit sleepy when two crazy things happened: first, Jesus's face started to shine like the sun and his clothes became dazzling white. Then Moses and Elijah, two superheroes of the Old Testament, appeared and began to talk with Jesus! To top it all off, God the Father spoke to them from a cloud, saying, "This is my beloved son, with whom I am well pleased; listen to him!" The disciples were not sleepy any longer, but terrified! Moses and Elijah disappeared, Jesus went back to normal, and then told them, "Tell no one of what you have seen." He's gotta be kidding!

Jesus wanted to give these disciples a glimpse of the glory to come. He knew that their faith in him would be shaken once he was forced to take up his cross. Kids, fear not: this cross leads to resurrection.

Ora et Labora

- It can be difficult for some to focus on God's goodness when life is challenging. Let's pray for those undergoing a difficult time in their life, that God may give them a glimpse of the glory to come.

- Peter, James, and John were blessed to be at Jesus's side at important times in his ministry. Reach out to a Christian friend or two in your own life and send them a note of encouragement for a fruitful Lent.

Deep Dive

- Moses and Elijah represented two very important things to the Jews of Jesus's time: the Law and the Prophets. Moses was given the law on Mt. Sinai, and Elijah was one of the most well-known prophets in the Old Testament.

March 13—RCIA

"Repent and be baptized every one of you in the name of Jesus Christ for the forgiveness of your sins, and you will receive the gift of the Holy Spirit."
(Acts 2:38)

Dear children, many of you became Catholic before you could even walk. Your parents brought you forward to receive the saving waters of baptism when you were a tiny baby. But have you ever wondered how people become Catholic when they're grown up and too big for their parents to hold? They go through a process at your parish called the RCIA.

RCIA stands for the Rite of Christian Initiation for Adults. When a person is deciding if they want to be a disciple for Christ, they can sign up for the RCIA process at a parish, and learn about the Catholic faith. They learn the teachings of the Church, how to pray, and how to follow Jesus. During the Lenten season we'll be able to share in the final part of their journey into the faith. The Church has three steps called the Scrutinies that the RCIA candidates undertake on the final three Sundays of Lent. If they continue through Lent and decide they indeed do want to become Catholic, they'll be able to receive the sacraments at the Easter Vigil liturgy.

Kids, this is really exciting for them and for your whole parish community! Let's strengthen them by our prayers and prepare to welcome them into the Body of Christ.

Ora et Labora

- Let's pray for those in the RCIA and their families!

- If your parents think it would be appropriate, contact the parish and see if you can find a catechumen to "adopt." This would be an opportunity to pray for a person in particular, let them know of your support, and prepare to welcome them into your parish.

Deep Dive

- The Church has prepared catechumens for baptism during this pre-Easter time for many centuries, and has long used the Easter Vigil as the time to initiate new members.

March 14—Abraham

God said, "I will establish my covenant as an everlasting covenant between me and you and your descendants after you for the generations to come, to be your God and the God of your descendants after you."
(Genesis 17:7)

In the New Testament, Abraham is called the "Father of Faith." But by the time he became an actual father, he was older than most grandfathers!

Abraham and his wife, Sarah, loved God and were faithful to him. But, despite many years of trying, they could not have any children. But one evening God asked Abraham to look up at the night sky and told him that he would have as many descendants as the stars. At this point, Abraham and his wife were quite old...how could they have even ONE child, much less one that could spawn an entire nation? But they trusted God and he blessed them with a child: Isaac. We'll hear more about him later.

Because of the great faith of Abraham, God entered into a covenant with him. God made Abraham the father of this great nation of Israel, from which came holy men such as Moses, David, and eventually the King of Kings: Jesus.

Ora et Labora

- Many married couples suffer greatly while bearing the cross of infertility. Let's pray that God may make his presence known in their trials.

- St. Paul calls Abraham the "Father of Faith." St. Paul also reminds us of the importance of "faith working through love." Show your faith today by making a concrete act of love for someone in your life.

Deep Dive

- Abraham is very unique as he is a respected figure in three major faith traditions: Judaism, Christianity, and Islam.

March 15—Baptism

"We were buried therefore with him by baptism into death, in order that, just as Christ was raised from the dead by the glory of the Father, we too might walk in newness of life."
(Romans 6:4)

Have you ever been to the baptism of a little baby? A non-Christian might watch this event unfold and not see what the big deal is. After the priest pours the water over the baby's head, it doesn't look like much has changed. The baby looks the same, smells the same, even cries the same way. But they are NOT the same.

We Catholics make a big deal about baptism. Why, you say? Well, the Church tells us that this is how Jesus's saving death on the cross is applied to each one of us. This is how we become God's children, how we join his Church, and how we are cleansed of original sin. It also prepares us for heaven. We make a big deal out of it because it IS a big deal!

During Lent, baptism should be on our mind. Many people are making their final preparations in RCIA to receive these saving waters and to join our Church family. Let's continue to pray for them!

Ora et Labora

- Let's keep praying for our catechumens, those preparing for baptism. They may be attacked by doubts, obstacles, and distractions to keep them away from the holy waters. Let's strengthen them with our prayers!

- If you don't already, start celebrating the baptismal anniversaries of the people in your family. These are like our "spiritual birthdays." On our birthday, we celebrate the day we were born; on our spiritual birthday we celebrate the day we were reborn!

Deep Dive

- Baptism is one of the seven sacraments; it's also known as the gateway to the other sacraments. A person becomes a Christian through baptism and only then is able to receive the other channels of grace that the Church offers.

March 16—Repentance and Conversion

"Repent and be baptized every one of you in the name of
Jesus Christ for the forgiveness of your sins, and you will
receive the gift of the Holy Spirit."
(Acts 2:38)

There's a saying that goes like this: "Love means never having to say you're sorry." This just isn't true, kids. Love means having to say you're sorry a LOT.

We humans are a fallen race. That means that we're tempted to sin often, and darn it, we do sin, nearly every day. This could cause us to despair, but don't. God asks us to do two simple things in the midst of our sin: repent and convert.

Repentance is expressing how sorry we are that we sinned. It's tough to admit that we messed up, but so necessary. The next part can be just as tough: conversion. This is when we turn away from that sin and run towards God. How often do we have to repent and convert? Oh gosh, every single day. And with God's grace, we can do just that.

Ora et Labora

- Sometimes we commit a sin…and we don't really feel that bad about it! Let's pray that the Lord will reveal to us the gravity of our sins, but also give us a glimpse of his eternal mercy.

- Making a regular examination of conscience is important to make sure we're on the right spiritual path. Do this at least once a week…and make sure to get to confession during Lent! (Here is an examination of conscience based on the Ten Commandments: https://amazingcatechists.com/2014/11/examination-of-conscience-for-kids/)

Deep Dive

- Conversion is from a Latin word that means "to turn." When we convert, we literally turn away from sin and head towards the Lord.

March 17—St. Patrick

God has given me the grace to be a minister of Jesus Christ to the nations.
(Romans 15:15-16)

Think of the last time that you were dragged to a place you didn't want to go, had a terrible experience, and then, when you got home, said to yourself, "I can't wait to go back!" Well, that is exactly what happened to St. Patrick.

Though the Irish claim this saint as their own, he wasn't born in Ireland. He grew up in what we now know as Scotland, was kidnapped at age 16 by pirates, and was sold to an Irish landowner who forced him to work as a shepherd. Though life was difficult, he found faith in God and prayed almost constantly. He escaped after six years in captivity and returned to his homeland. He desired, however, to return to Ireland and spread the good news of Jesus Christ.

Twenty years later, after becoming a bishop, he was sent back to Ireland to preach to the people of that pagan land. He worked hard to end the system of slavery that had held him captive all those years. Patrick converted thousands to the faith, often using the three-leafed shamrock to help explain the Holy Trinity.

He died in 462 AD and the Irish people immediately hailed him as a saint. Though his feast day always falls in the midst of Lent, this is always a great day of celebration for those with an Irish heritage!

Ora et Labora

- Let's pray for the Irish people and those of Irish descent today.

- Wear green, eat Irish food and dance a jig, but don't forget that living the Christian life every day is the best way to honor this great saint.

Deep Dive

- A wonderful prayer from this great saint is called the Lorica of St. Patrick. This excerpt would be a wonderful morning prayer to have hanging on your wall:

I sing as I arise today,
I call upon the Father's might;
The will of God to be my guide,
The eye of God to be my sight.

The word of God to be my speech,
The hand of God to be my stay;
The shield of God to be my strength,
The path of God to be my way.

March 18—Passion Figures

A large number of people followed him, including women
who mourned and wailed for him.
(Luke 23:27)

I often think about how alone Jesus must have felt on his way to the cross. Think of all the people in the crowd who were jeering and spitting on him. But he was not alone. There were people along the way to share his burdens with.

There was Veronica, the woman who tenderly wiped the blood and sweat away from his face. There was Simon, the reluctant man who helped Jesus carry his cross. There was John, the beloved disciple, and his mother Mary, who stayed at the foot of the cross until his last breath.

We have people in our lives right now who are struggling with their own crosses and need our help to bear them. And they in turn can help us bear ours.

Ora et Labora

- There are many in our world who are unjustly imprisoned and condemned to death. Let's pray for them, their families, and for their ultimate vindication.

- Who are the people around you that are carrying a heavy burden right now? How can you help them lighten their load?

Deep Dive

- It is said that, when Veronica wiped the face of Jesus, it left an image of his face on the cloth. The name Veronica means "true image."

March 19—St. Joseph

As for me and my house, we will serve the Lord.
(Joshua 24:15)

Question: Who is the father of Jesus?

If you answered "God," you would be right. If you answered "Joseph," you would also be right!

Joseph was a righteous man, a carpenter who was betrothed to a young lady named Mary. When he discovered that she was pregnant before they were together, he thought it would be best if he divorced her quietly. An angel, however, came to him in a dream and told him to be not afraid, for this child was conceived by the Holy Spirit. I think it's fair to say that Joseph was a bit confused, but he trusted God and took Mary into his home.

Joseph became the foster father of Jesus; he was there when the child was born in Bethlehem, he took Jesus and Mary to Egypt when Herod came to slay the young children, and then brought his family back to Nazareth when the angel said that it was safe to return. He raised and protected Jesus until he grew to maturity. Tradition tells us that Joseph died in the arms of Jesus and Mary, the Holy Family together one last time.

This is a great feast day in the Church, and we get to celebrate it in Lent! Live it up today!

Ora et Labora

- Pray for any friends of your family that are preparing for marriage or fatherhood. Pray also for any of your friends without a father.

- St. Joseph is the patron saint of fathers, so spend time with your dad today and ask St. Joseph to intercede for him!

Deep Dive

- Some think that Joseph was a young husband, while others believe that he was an old widower when he was wed to Mary.

March 20—The Woman at The Well

"If you knew the gift of God and who it is that asks you for a drink, you would have asked him and he would have given you living water."
(John 4:10)

There are three special readings from John's Gospel that we'll see in the coming weeks that were specially selected for our catechumens preparing for baptism. The first one is about a woman at a well who had an encounter that would change her life forever.

When they both met at the well to get water, this Samaritan woman was astonished when Jesus began talking to her. The Jews and the Samaritans were mortal enemies, not to mention that this woman herself was an outcast by her own community because of the many husbands she had had. But there are no outcasts to Jesus. Everyone is worthy of God's mercy and compassion. Instead of the water she was taking from the well, he offers her the gift of living water by which she will never thirst again.

Kids, we have people right now in our parishes seeking that living water flowing from God's grace: the waters of baptism. The woman at the well is so changed by Jesus that she dashes back into town to tell everyone about this man who knew everything about her. Let us go and do likewise.

Ora et Labora

- Whenever you feel thirsty today, say a quick prayer for the catechumens in your parish before you take a drink.

- Show your love for your family by filling up their water glasses before meal times this week.

Deep Dive

- In the Eastern churches, the woman at the well is revered as saint. She is known by the name Photine, which means "the enlightened one."

March 21—Moses

*"If you will indeed obey my voice and keep my covenant, you
shall be my treasured possession among all peoples, for all
the earth is mine; and you shall be to me a kingdom of priests
and a holy nation," says the Lord.
(Exodus 19:5-6)*

Ah yes, the great Moses. He was so cool that, when he was
just a shepherd, God revealed his sacred name to Moses. And God
doesn't name-drop himself to just anyone!

Moses had a very interesting life: he was raised in luxury by
the Egyptian Pharaoh, but killed a man and had to flee. He became a
shepherd. One day God revealed himself to Moses in a burning bush
and called him to lead the Israelites out of Egypt. And Moses did just
that. Their journey out of Egypt is called the Exodus.

After he had rescued them from the clutches of the Pharaoh,
God wanted to renew his covenant with the Hebrew people. He
called Moses up to the top of Mount Sinai and appeared to him in
fire, an earthquake, and a cloud. I'm sure Moses was a little nervous!
God told Moses that he would make a great nation of the Israelite
people, and handed Moses two tablets of stone that would guide
them for centuries to come. On those tablets were the Ten
Commandments.

Moses wandered in the desert with the Israelites for 40 years.
He led his people to the Promised Land, but, sadly, was unable to
enter with them. Before Moses died, he told of a great prophet who
would rise up after him. This prophet was Jesus, who one day would
make an everlasting covenant with his people.

Ora et Labora

- We often think about slavery as something from the past, but
  it still exists today in many parts of the world. Let's pray for

those who are enslaved and for the people who work to free them.

- Moses was a great leader because he trusted in God and worked to live a life of holiness. Kids, be life Moses and strive to live virtuously every day!

Deep Dive

- God revealed his name to Moses as YHWH, usually pronounced as "Yah-weh." It means "I-Am-Who-I-Am." If you want to impress your friends, the four letters of God's name are often referred to as the *tetragrammaton*.

March 22—The Ten Commandments

So (Moses) was there with the Lord forty days and forty nights. He neither ate bread nor drank water. And he wrote on the tablets the words of the covenant, the Ten Commandments.
(Exodus 34:28)

Here's something that Christians and Jews have in common: we both love God's Commandments. We also have a hard time following them perfectly!

After he helped Moses bring the Israelites out of Egypt, God was determined to help his people live in the freedom of his love. And so he gave Moses ten instructions to share with them. Thousands of years later, they are still a foundation for our moral life. The first three are about loving God, and the next seven are about loving our neighbor. Here they are:

1. I am the LORD your God: you shall not have strange Gods before me.

2. You shall not take the name of the LORD your God in vain.

3. Remember to keep holy the LORD'S Day.

_____

4. Honor your father and your mother.

5. You shall not kill.

6. You shall not commit adultery.

7. You shall not steal.

8. You shall not bear false witness against your neighbor.

9. You shall not covet your neighbor's wife.

10. You shall not covet your neighbor's goods.

Some of these are easier for kids to keep. Some are harder! Unfortunately, many people see these Commandments as burdensome. They're not supposed to be. Instead, let's look at them the way God intended, as guideposts to keep us from sin and freeing us to live as his sons and daughters.

Ora et Labora

- Which of the Commandments is the hardest for you? Take it to prayer and ask God for special graces to overcome those difficulties.

- Memorize the Ten Commandments! They are also a great tool to make a good examination of conscience before going to the Sacrament of Reconciliation.

Deep Dive

- The Ten Commandments are often referred to as the Decalogue, which means "the ten words." The Jewish people and other Christian denominations actually number the commandments a little differently than Catholics and Lutherans do, since they are not numbered in the Bible passages themselves. (cf. Exodus 20 and Deuteronomy 5)

March 23—The Prodigal Son

"This son of mine was dead and is alive again; he was lost and is found."
(Luke 15:24)

The Jewish people have always considered pigs to be unclean animals. They don't eat them, they don't have them as pets...they just don't like them. So think about how humiliating it would be for a Jewish man to wallow in the mud with a bunch of pigs, feeding them while he himself was nearly starving.

Jesus told a story about a man with two sons. The younger son told his father that he wanted his inheritance now. He received it and went far away. The son quickly blew all his money on foolish things and became so desperate that he had to take a job feeding pigs. Finally he told himself, "Why am I doing this? My father has more than enough. I will get up, go home, and ask my father to take me back, no longer as a son, but as his servant."

His father had been watching everyday, waiting for his son's return. When he saw his prodigal son returning from afar, he ran to him, embraced him, and prepared a great feast for him. Most importantly, he welcomed him back not as a servant, as the son had hoped for, but as his beloved child once again.

Kids, this is what happens every time we turn from our sins and come back to the Father. He welcomes us home with open arms, rejoices with his angels and saints, and restores us as his sons and daughters. Let's thank God for his great mercy and love!

Ora et Labora

- St. John said, "We are God's children now." (1 John 3:2) The fatherhood of God can be difficult to embrace, however, for those who grew up without a dad. Let's pray for those with an orphan's heart, that they may experience the Father's love.

- Think of the son's joy when he was embraced by his father; never discount the power of a hug! Be generous with your hugs today.

Deep Dive

- The word "prodigal" means "spending money recklessly."

March 24—Reconciliation

All this is from God, who reconciled us to himself through
Christ and gave us the ministry of reconciliation.
(2 Corinthians 5:18)

I've got good news, kids: there is no sin too big that God can't forgive. The bad news: We gotta fess up to it. Well, confess up to it, I guess.

Jesus was smart. He knew full well that we would keep messing up even after receiving his grace in baptism. To help us out, he empowered his Apostles to forgive sins, so we could again be reconciled to the Father. And fortunately for us, our priests have that same ability to forgive our sins through the grace of God. The Sacrament of Reconciliation is a sacrament of healing. And we need to be healed. Mankind has a fallen nature, and because of this we continually run away from Christ and his Church through our sin. But Jesus always calls us back, no matter how many times we've strayed. He invites us into the confessional so that we might admit our sins and show our sorrow for them. He then pours out his mercy and restores us in his grace.

Think again about the prodigal son. He messed up big time, but recognized his sinfulness, returned to his father, confessed his sin, and was welcomed back into his family. We can do the same!

Ora et Labora

- Make an examination of conscience a regular part of your prayer. Digging deep to find our hidden sins helps to expose them to God's healing light.

- Get to confession before Easter!

Deep Dive

- As you probably learned in your preparation for this sacrament, there are four elements of reconciliation:
  - Contrition: Feeling sorrow for sin
  - Confession: Telling your sins to the priest
  - Absolution: The priest forgives your sins
  - Satisfaction: Righting the wrongs that we have done through prayer or action

March 25—Annunciation

The Lord himself will give you this sign: the virgin shall be with child, and bear a son, and shall name him Emmanuel. (Isaiah 7:14)

Boy, this seems like a strange feast to celebrate in the middle of Lent. Why today for the Annunciation? Well, babies are in their mother's womb for nine months, and guess what is nine months from today? Christmas!

One day, the angel Gabriel came to the young maiden, Mary, and greeted her with, "Hail, full of grace, the Lord is with thee." Mary was most assuredly surprised by this messenger from heaven, and probably a little nervous. He tells her to "be not afraid," that she would conceive a son, would name him Jesus, and that he would reign as king over the house of Jacob forever. All this to a 13-year-old girl who still lived with her parents!

St. Bernard of Clairvaux said that "all creation held its breath, awaiting her reply." The entire work of our salvation hinged on her response to the angel Gabriel! Although Mary didn't fully understand his plan, she trusted God and said, "Be it done unto me according to thy word." And it was!

Ora et Labora

- The *Angelus* is a wonderful devotion that helps us ponder the Annunciation. Pray it today at one of the times that it is traditionally said: 6:00 AM, Noon, and 6 PM. It only takes a minute! (You can find it here: https://www.usccb.org/prayers/angelus)

- Although this is a Friday in Lent, this wonderful feast day cancels out our usual Lenten penances. So take advantage and feast!

Deep Dive

- When a person is given a special calling in the Bible, they are often given a new name. In the Old Testament, Abram became Abraham. In the New Testament, Simon was given the name Peter. At the angel's greeting, Mary, too, was given a new name: *kecharitomene* (kay-CAR-ee-toh-me-nay), a Greek word that means, "one who is full of grace."

March 26—The Man Born Blind

"One thing I do know. I was blind but now I see!"
(John 9:25)

Today we'll explore another story from John's Gospel that the Church specially chose for our catechumens preparing for baptism. It's a story about a man being healed, but he probably wasn't thrilled with what Jesus had to rub on his eyes to do it!

In Jesus's time, many people thought that if you were blind or deaf, one of your parents had brought that upon you by their own sins. God therefore had punished you for their mistakes. One day the Pharisees asked Jesus about a particular blind man in the town: who had sinned in his case? Jesus said that this man was blind not because of his parents, but so that God's great works could be shown to all. Jesus spat on the ground and mixed it with dirt. He rubbed that mud on the man's eyes and sent him to be washed in a nearby pool. When the man emerged from the water, he could see!

The Church gives us this reading in Lent so that we may see the connection to baptism. Our RCIA candidates are preparing to receive those baptismal waters that remove spiritual blindness. The eyes of their hearts will be enlightened, released from darkness, prisoners of sin no longer. They can say with that blind man, "I was blind, but now I see."

Ora et Labora

- We're getting closer to Easter. Keep praying for our RCIA candidates! If you know one of them personally, reach out to encourage them today.

- Try an experiment: close your eyes and ask one of your family members to lead you around the house or your yard for a few minutes. Imagine how challenging it must be to do that your whole life, but then also imagine how joyful that man must have been to gain his sight!

Deep Dive

- In the early Church, the sacrament of baptism was often known as "illumination" or "enlightenment."

March 27—Laetare Sunday

"Rejoice with Jerusalem, and be glad for her, all you who love her; rejoice with her in joy, all you who mourn over her."
(Isaiah 66:10)

Just like in Advent, we have another "Rejoice" Sunday in the middle of a liturgical season. After 3.5 weeks of our Lenten fasts, we probably need a day like this to remind us what we're working toward!

Today is "Laetare (Lay-TAHR-rey) Sunday," the traditional halfway point of Lent. Our priest's vestments will be rose, a mix of penitential purple and the joyful white of Easter. And why this joy in the middle of our penitential season? Because we know how this story ends: at an empty tomb, with death destroyed. This day can be a little break in our Lenten fasts, if you want, to give us a foretaste of the Easter feast to come.

Our Bible verse today exhorts us to rejoice not by ourselves, but with the great city of Jerusalem. In the Bible, Jerusalem represents heaven, but also our Holy Mother Church here on earth. Kids, let us rejoice this day with the Church in heaven and here on earth.

Ora et Labora

- Spring is a very difficult time for those who suffer from depression and the dangers that go with it. Let's pray for those who bear that cross, that the Lord will place joy in their hearts.

- Today is also known as "Mothering Sunday" in some countries, a day to recognize the Church as our mother. People would often travel to the church of their baptism for a special service. As a possible alternative, how about doing something nice for your own mother instead!

Deep Dive

- Many years ago, certain Sundays in the Church year were identified by the opening word of the entrance chant (called an "Introit") sung at the beginning of Mass. "Laetare" is the first word of the Introit for this Fourth Sunday of Lent, hence "Laetare Sunday."

March 28—Exodus

He brought them out of darkness and the shadow of death,
and broke their chains in pieces.
(Psalm 107:14)

Remember the story of Moses and the Israelites escaping from Egypt? Pharaoh said they could leave, but then changed his mind and sent his entire army after them. And they weren't coming to talk; they were coming to kill.

The Israelites had been enslaved for centuries, but God had decided that it was time for them to be free. He called upon Moses to tell Pharaoh that he must release them. When Pharaoh refused, God sent ten plagues that devastated the Egyptians. Finally, Pharaoh relented. He let the Hebrew people go. They left...but then came Pharaoh's army after them. Once the Israelites reached the shores of the Red Sea, all hope seemed lost. They were trapped between the water and the army. But God sent a great wind that blew back the waters of the sea, allowing them to cross over to the other side. When they made it safely across, the waters came crashing back, drowning the Egyptian soldiers. The Hebrew people were free at last!

The Church has always seen Easter as a spiritual exodus. We were like the Israelites, longing to be free not from Pharaoh, but from the bonds of sin and death. Jesus is the new Moses who leads his people out of the slavery of sin. We pass through the waters of baptism, just as the Hebrews passed through the Red Sea. And as the Israelites were assured of the Promised Land by God, we, too, are given the pledge of the promised land of Heaven. Our catechumens are preparing to undergo this exodus in their own lives. Let's pray for them!

Ora et Labora

- Many people in our world are fleeing their home countries to find better lives for their families. Let's pray for their safety and wellbeing.

- Find a new family on the block, or a new kid in school, and let them know they are welcome and appreciated.

Deep Dive

- Exodus is from a Greek word that means "the way out." The second book in the Old Testament is entitled Exodus.

March 29—David

"When your days are over and you rest with your ancestors, I will raise up your offspring to succeed you, your own flesh and blood, and I will establish his kingdom," says the Lord.
(2 Samuel 7:12)

Many of you first heard about David as the brave young boy that slew the giant Goliath with a slingshot. Well, that little boy grew up to be the greatest king that the nation of Israel ever knew. Okay, okay...the SECOND greatest.

When David grew up and became king, the army he led won many battles and made Israel a very powerful nation. As king, he ruled wisely and justly. David decided that the Ark of the Covenant, a large wooden chest covered with gold and containing the Ten Commandments, needed a magnificent home. He wanted to build a great temple in the city of Jerusalem where the Ark could be placed, and people could come to worship the Lord. God was pleased with this and relayed a message to David. He would make a new covenant with him: God would establish a great kingdom for the offspring of David, and his throne would be established forever.

Guess who that offspring is? Well, King Solomon was the son of David, and Solomon built the temple after David died. But God was referring to an even greater descendant of David, Jesus Christ, who was himself the temple of God. Jesus is the son of David, and the son of God, he whose kingdom will never end.

Ora et Labora

- Find Psalm 89 in your Bible and read the first 18 verses as part of your prayer today.

- Jesus has shared his roles of priest, prophet, and king with us, the baptized faithful. Find an act to do today that reflects one of the highest attributes of a good king and leader: service.

Deep Dive

- About half of the 150 psalms in the Bible are attributed to David. He was thought to have been a skilled musician and composed the psalms to be sung.

March 30—The Jesus Prayer

(The tax collector) would not even look up to heaven, but
beat his breast and said, "God, have mercy on me, a sinner."
(Luke 18:13)

Okay, kids, you're about to learn the shortest prayer ever which not only manages to glorify God, but also reminds us that we need him badly.

Jesus once told a parable about a Pharisee and a tax collector who went to the temple to pray. Pharisees were considered holy men, while tax collectors were seen as greedy, evil men by the Jewish people. The Pharisee prayed and said, "God, I thank you that I am not like other people—robbers, evildoers, adulterers—or even like this tax collector." He was very prideful, clearly. The tax collector, however, professed his humility and need for God by saying, "God, have mercy on me, a sinner."

From this parable we get this amazing prayer, short but powerful:

Lord Jesus Christ, Son of the living God, have mercy on me, a sinner.

It's called the "Jesus Prayer" and it's perfect for Lent! Let's never forget the humility our Lord took on for our salvation, and our great need for his mercy.

Ora et Labora

- This prayer is so easy to memorize. Do so! Then pray it frequently in this Lenten season.

- Sometimes we think that we need to criticize others for their failings to make us feel better about ourselves. Instead, when you find yourself thinking about the flaws of another person in your life, focus on the fact that they are profoundly loved by God, too. And then do something kind for them!

Deep Dive

- In the Latin Mass, nearly everything is in the Latin language, obviously. One exception is the *Kyrie Eleison*, which is in Greek. It translates as "Lord, have mercy." You can see its connection to Jesus's parable mentioned above.

March 31—The Woman Caught in Adultery

Jesus said, "Go, and sin no more."
(John 8:11)

Many of the religious leaders 2000 years ago shared something in common: they thought Jesus was a real nuisance. He was always pointing out their hypocrisies, and calling them to repent. And so they were constantly trying to put Jesus in tricky situations so they could trap him. And it always backfired.

When Jesus was in the Temple for a Jewish feast, the scribes and Pharisees brought to him a woman they had caught in adultery, a very serious sin. The religious leaders said to Jesus, "The law of Moses commands us to stone adulterous women to death. What do you say?" They were trying to trap Jesus with this dilemma. If Jesus said to stone her, it would contradict all his teaching about God's mercy to sinners. But if he said not to stone her, the Jews would say that he didn't follow the law of Moses. He was in a tight spot! Jesus turned it around on them, however, by saying, "Whoever among you has never sinned, let them throw the first stone." That certainly made the scribes and Pharisees squirm! And so, ashamed of their own failings, all the religious leaders walked away one by one.

But what would Jesus say to the woman? When they were alone, he said to her, "I do not condemn you. Go, and sin no more." This woman, who was minutes away from being stoned to death, could now rise up, and begin her new life, forgiven and freed by Jesus.

Ora et Labora

- Adultery often leads to troubled relationships. Let's pray for strong, faithful marriages today.

- We've been called to show the same mercy to others that Jesus showed to the adulterous woman. Be quick to forgive a parent, friend, or sibling today!

Deep Dive

- The Bible tells us that Jesus was writing on the ground while the Pharisees were questioning him. We don't know what he was writing, but some of the Church Fathers speculated that Jesus may have been listing the sins of those who had brought the woman before him.

April 1—The Sorrowful Mysteries of the Rosary

I have been crucified with Christ. It is no longer I who live,
but Christ who lives in me.
(Galatians 2:20)

The suffering that our Lord endured on that Good Friday long ago is beyond anything we can imagine. We know he did this for us...but why do we need to dwell on it so much? It's really hard to think about Jesus's death on the cross; what good is it to keep reminding us about it?

One set of mysteries for the rosary certainly won't let us forget about what he underwent for our salvation. The Sorrowful mysteries not only walk us through each step of his journey, but also ask us to meditate on them, to really ponder what that road to the cross was like. There are five of them:

1. The Agony in the Garden

2. The Scourging at the Pillar

3. The Crowning with Thorns

4. The Carrying of the Cross

5. The Crucifixion

The Church tells us that there is great value to our lives to live with these mysteries, praying over them with our blessed Mother through the rosary. But again: why? Well, to remind us that our sins came with a great price that only Jesus could pay. And to help us remember that our own Christian journey is not always an easy one. We have our own crosses to carry, our own sufferings for the kingdom of God. Let's follow the example of our Lord in all these things.

Ora et Labora

- Find time to pray at least part of the rosary in this Lenten season. A whole rosary can be challenging for kids, but even one mystery every day can help sanctify this time of year.

- Ask your parents about times they've carried heavy crosses in their lives. Maybe they'll be able to share some blessings that have come from them, too.

Deep Dive

- Usually the Sorrowful Mysteries are prayed on Tuesdays and Fridays. There is, however, an older tradition that assigns them to each day of Lent.

April 2—Lazarus

Jesus said to (Martha), "I am the resurrection and the life. Those who believe in me, even though they die, will live." (John 11:25)

Today we'll talk about the famous story of Jesus raising Lazarus from the dead. Unsurprisingly, the people standing around were probably holding their noses while it was happening. People who have been dead for four days do NOT smell good.

Word got to Jesus that his friend Lazarus had died. He traveled to the town of Bethany, where Lazarus and his sisters, Mary and Martha, lived. Martha was upset and questioned why Jesus hadn't come sooner so he could have saved her brother. But she also expressed her trust in Jesus, that he was the Christ, the Son of God. Jesus then went to the tomb, had the stone taken away, and then cried, "Lazarus, come out!" And Lazarus did! He was still tied up in his burial cloths, and probably not smelling his best...but he was ALIVE!

Kids, it may not seem like it, but this story is about baptism in a way. Jesus called Lazarus out of death and darkness, and raised him to new life. In baptism, we are called out of the darkness of sin to rise from the waters into new life with Christ. And this is just what our catechumens in RCIA are preparing for. Let's keep them in our prayers!

Ora et Labora

- Let's pray for those mourning the death of a loved one today.

- Ask your parents if you can have a Mass offered for a deceased family member. It would require a trip to the parish office and a small stipend.

Deep Dive

- When our Lord heard about the death of his friend, Lazarus, John the Evangelist wrote the shortest sentence in the Bible: "Jesus wept." (John 11:35)

April 3—Passion Sunday

Rejoice insofar as you share Christ's sufferings, that you may
also rejoice and be glad when his glory is revealed.
(1 Peter 4:13)

Sometimes you'll hear people talking about a "passion" they
have for something. A person may have a passion for baseball,
dancing, or woodworking. And it doesn't mean that they just like it;
we would say that it's something they love so much that it's worthy
of their blood, sweat, and tears.

This Sunday is traditionally known as Passion Sunday, a day
on which we start to focus our eyes more keenly on the cross of
Christ. And why do we call what Jesus faced on his road to Calvary
his Passion? Well, the Latin root of the word passion is *passio*,
which means "suffering." And you know what? Suffering is a part of
love. Athletes exercise strenuously to get better at the sport they
love. Actors work hard, repeating their lines over and over again to
hone their craft for the love of the stage. And Jesus endured the
jeers, the spitting, the nails, the spear, the cross for love of us.

This week we'll look at some examples from the Old
Testament that foreshadowed the Passion of Christ, giving the
Jewish people clues about the redeemer that was to come. Through
our reflections on his suffering and death, we may better understand
God's great passion for us.

Ora et Labora

- Let's pray for those who have particularly heavy burdens that
  they are carrying right now.

- Jesus said that we would have to take up our own crosses if
  we wished to be his disciples. "Taking up our cross" means
  that we have to live out our Christian life with courage and
  conviction, even the parts of it that are difficult. Identify one

aspect of your faith that feels like a cross to bear right now, and "offer it up" for love of the Lord.

Deep Dive

- There is a long tradition in the Church of covering up crosses and other sacred images from today until Holy Saturday, a type of "fasting of the eyes." If you have the means to do this in your house, this is an excellent way to prepare our hearts for the upcoming Holy Week.

April 4—Isaac

And Abraham said, "God himself will provide the lamb for a burnt offering, my son."
(Genesis 22:8)

Remember Abraham? God had said that he would make Abraham's descendants as numerous as the stars...but then God wanted him to sacrifice his only son. Abraham must have been so confused.

When Isaac was still a young lad, God sent his angel to Abraham. The angel told Abraham that he must sacrifice Isaac as a burnt offering to God. Abraham, I'm sure, was heartbroken at the thought, but he had always trusted God and he wasn't going to stop now. Abraham and Isaac traveled together up Mt. Moriah. Abraham placed the wood upon the shoulders of Isaac to carry, while Abraham brought the fire and the knife. Isaac didn't know what was to happen. He asked his father, "Where is the lamb for the sacrifice?" Abraham said that God would provide the lamb for sacrifice. When they reached the summit, Isaac was placed on the altar. And just as Abraham raised his knife, the angel of the Lord appeared and told him to stop, and not kill the child. God had tested Abraham and he had obeyed. He would indeed see his many blessings through his descendants.

Kids, let me know if any of this sounds familiar: a father's only-begotten son goes up a hill carrying wood on his shoulders so that he may make of himself a sacrificial offering to the Father. Yep, you got it: Isaac walked the same path that Jesus would centuries later. The big difference? Jesus would indeed be sacrificed on the wood of the cross, the ultimate offering for our sins.

Ora et Labora

- Let's pray for parents who have suffered the loss of a child.

- Isaac certainly would have noticed his father's unease as they traveled up the mountain. When you notice one of your parents having a difficult day, be quick to take on an extra chore to show that you care.

Deep Dive

- King Solomon built his great temple on the same mountain on which Isaac and Abraham climbed. Not far from this mountain is Calvary, where our Lord was crucified.

April 5—The Suffering Servant

He was despised and rejected by men; a man of sorrows,
acquainted with grief.
(Isaiah 53:3)

Today we'll look at another figure from the Old Testament. This person predicted some of the trials that our Lord would have to undergo on Good Friday. He is the Suffering Servant written about by Isaiah.

Near the end of the book of Isaiah, the prophet speaks about a "man of sorrows." This man made of himself an offering to God for the sins of the people, though they had despised and rejected him. They were like sheep who had gone astray, each going their own way. But for love of them, this Suffering Servant became like a lamb himself being led to the slaughter. And yet he opened not his mouth in protest as he endured his trials. Isaiah said that this Suffering Servant was wounded for our transgressions, and that he healed us by the stripes he bore on his bloodied back.

Kids, this was written hundreds of years before Christ was born. What an astounding prophecy about our Lord Jesus who laid down his life for the sins of his people. He endured suffering and death because of our transgressions, and he carried our griefs and sorrows with him to the cross. And when he hung on it, from his mouth came not curses, but words of forgiveness.

Ora et Labora

- Millions of Christians worldwide suffer persecution for their faith, even in our modern age. Let's pray for those who are persecuted today.

- Never allow a moment of suffering in our lives to be wasted! When you endure a trial, offer a prayer that God will use that suffering for the good of the world.

Deep Dive

- This section of Isaiah was written when the Jewish people had been conquered by the Babylonians and kicked out of the Promised Land. Some Jews saw the Suffering Servant of Isaiah as their nation of Israel itself, beaten and wounded by their enemies.

April 6—The Righteous Man

If the righteous man is God's son, he will help him, and will deliver him from the hand of his adversaries.
(Wisdom 2:18)

The book of Wisdom is a lesser known book of the Bible, and for some of our Protestant brothers and sisters it's a completely unknown one...since their Bibles don't even have it! But if we overlook this book, we miss out on an incredible prophecy of the Passion of our Lord.

In Wisdom chapter two, the author speaks of the wicked, those who fulfill their own desires while oppressing the poor and the weak. Though they have all that they could seemingly want, they are bothered by the presence of a righteous man. They rant and rave how this man calls himself a child of the Lord and avoids the ways of sin. The wicked can't stand such a man, so they decide to insult him, torture him, and condemn him to a shameful death. "If he is truly a son of God," they say, "he will be protected."

On one hand, it's no surprise that the early Church Fathers read this as a prediction of Christ and his suffering at the hands of evil men. But the author of the book of Wisdom wants us to also know this: the wicked hate ALL those who are righteous, all those who are faithful, all those who profess to be children of God. That's us, kiddos. And the witness we bear to the crucified Lord comes with a cost. But it also comes with the promise of eternal glory.

Ora et Labora

- There are many people in prison right now who are innocent of the crimes they were accused of committing. Some are even awaiting execution. Let's pray for their families, and for their eventual exoneration.

- It's easy to find yourself with friends and start talking about others behind their back. This is something we should never participate in. When gossip starts up, change the subject, find an excuse to leave, or find something kind to say about the person who is being gossiped about.

Deep Dive

- Catholic Bibles have seven books that our Protestant brethren do not have in theirs. We call them the "detuterocanonical" books. They include the books of Tobit, Judith, Wisdom, Sirach, Baruch, and First and Second Maccabees.

April 7—Jeremiah

"For this is the (new) covenant that I will make with the house of Israel after those days," declares the Lord: "I will put my law within them, and I will write it on their hearts."
(Jeremiah 31:33)

Jeremiah, like many of the Old Testament prophets, was not well-liked. In fact, he made a lot of people mad, and it was no surprise. He was always talking about the need for the Jewish people to repent and obey the Lord. And that got him in trouble.

The Church Fathers saw a lot of similarities between the life of Jeremiah and the life of Jesus. Both were chosen by God from the womb, both called the people to conversion, and both made enemies with the Jewish leaders. Some officials became so angry with Jeremiah that they cast him into a deep well without any water, only mud. There Jeremiah surely would have died had he not been rescued by an Ethiopian servant of the king. Being cast into a dark pit and brought out again was another way that Jeremiah's journey echoed our Lord's. Remember that Jesus was cast into a dark tomb, but he, too, emerged again triumphantly.

The book of Jeremiah gives us a big clue into the Lord's plan for his faithful people. God revealed to Jeremiah that there would one day be a new covenant between God and Israel. There would be a new law for God's people that would not be written on tablets of stone, but on the hearts of the faithful. Hundreds of years later, this new covenant would be established with the blood of Christ. And we renew that new covenant with God every time we receive him in the Holy Eucharist.

Ora et Labora

- Let's pray for our priests, who, like Jeremiah, often have to preach some difficult truths to people who would prefer not to hear them.

- Think of how grateful Jeremiah must have been when a brave man pulled him out of that pit. Think of someone in your own life that is feeling trapped in a deep pit and give them some love and encouragement.

Deep Dive

- The biblical book of Lamentations is traditionally thought to have been written by the prophet Jeremiah. The Lamentations are sorrowful poems that reflect on the city of Jerusalem after it was destroyed by the Babylonians in 587 BC.

April 8—The Seven Last Words

"Father, forgive them for they do not know what they
are doing."
(Luke 23:34)

When a person is faced with death, they understand that time is limited and their final words to their loved ones matter. Jesus, struggling to breathe in his last moments on the cross, made sure to make his final words count.

The Church has long honored the final sayings of Jesus, and found great consolation in them. These are the Seven Last Words of Christ:

To those who put him on this cross, he interceded for them by saying, "Father, forgive them for they do not know what they are doing."

To the penitent thief who asked Jesus to remember him when he came into the kingdom of God, he said, "Indeed, I promise you, today you will be with Me in paradise."

To his mother Mary he entrusts his beloved disciple, John, saying, "Woman, behold your son."
And in turn he places Mary in John's care as he says, "Behold, your mother."

Feeling alone in his anguish, he cries out to the Father, saying, "My God, my God, why have you abandoned me?"

He longs to drink the cup of redemption that the Father has given him, so he says, "I thirst."

With his saving death near at hand, Jesus said, "It is finished."

Finally, he entrusts himself to our loving Lord, saying, "Father, into your hands I commend my spirit."

Even as he hung on that cross, Jesus thought first of others. He extended mercy to his tormentors. He tended to his mother and friend. And he journeyed into death to save his beloved people. Holy Week is almost here.

Ora et Labora

- Let's pray today for those who feel abandoned by God.

- As we prepare for Holy Week, consider adding another penance to your Lenten practice, or renewing one that has fallen by the wayside.

Deep Dive

- Matthew and Mark have only one "last word" in their Gospels, and it's the same one: "My God, my God, why have you abandoned me?" (Matthew 27:46; Mark 15:34) Luke and John have three apiece.

April 9—The Temple

Jesus said, "Destroy this temple and in three days I'll raise it up."
(John 2:19)

Kids, if someone asked you where God's house was, you might say heaven or that he lives at church. Well, the Jews in Jesus's time would have said that God dwells in the Temple in Jerusalem.

King Solomon built an enormous temple in the city of Jerusalem where the Ark of the Covenant could dwell, and the Jewish people could come and offer their sacrifices to God. It was replaced by another temple centuries later, and Jesus knew that one well. He was brought there as a baby at his Presentation, he called it his Father's house when he was a young boy, and he traveled there every year of his life to celebrate the Passover. And one Passover he became quite angry, and chased out those people who were treating the Temple as a place to scam those who came to worship. Jesus loved the Temple, but he also knew that it wouldn't last forever. It was destroyed by the Romans about forty years after Jesus died.

But if the Temple is gone, where now is God's holy presence? Where does he live? The Temple of God now is Jesus Christ himself. He gives us a clue to that reality when he tells those in the Temple, "Destroy this temple and in three days I'll raise it up." And since we are part of his body, we, too, are temples of his Holy Spirit. Let's offer our own sacrifices to God, not of animals, but of praise.

Ora et Labora

- Let's pray for those who cheat and lie to take advantage of others, and for their victims.

- As temples of the Holy Spirit, it's important that we keep our souls as clean as possible. Daily prayer, acts of love, and reception of the sacraments are keys to spiritual progress.

Deep Dive

- In the innermost part of the temple was the Holy of Holies, which contained the Ark of the Covenant. The Jewish high priest was only allowed to enter that room once a year to offer sacrifice, on the Day of Atonement.

April 10—Palm Sunday of the Lord's Passion

Behold, your king is coming to you; righteous and victorious, humble and mounted on a donkey...he will proclaim peace to the nations.
(Zechariah 9:9, 10)

Holy Week begins today! Let us turn our eyes this week to the holy city of Jerusalem and follow Jesus every step of the way.

The prophet Zechariah spoke of a righteous king that would ride on a donkey, proclaiming peace to the nations (Zech 9:9). I'm sure the Jews before Jesus's time were a bit confused by this prophecy, as kings were more likely to be riding around on great stallions.

As he prepared to enter Jerusalem for the last time, Jesus sent two of his disciples to a village up ahead; there they would find a colt that had never been ridden before. They brought the animal back with them and Jesus rode it into Jerusalem while the crowds laid down their cloaks and freshly-cut palms, acclaiming him with shouts of "Hosanna in the highest!" and, "Blessed is he who comes in the name of the Lord!" The great king, the prince of peace, riding on a donkey . . . the prophecy fulfilled!

At Mass today we hear this gospel proclaimed from the back of the church, then a great procession with our blessed palms . . . but things take a turn after that. Just a few minutes later, we hear the Passion being proclaimed. The prince of peace who was cheered by the crowds as he rode into town has now become the "King of the Jews," jeered by a mob who calls for his death.

Thus begins the holiest week of the year. Triumph and joy giving way to sorrow and tears.

Ora et Labora

- Discuss with your family why Jesus was cheered by some while others were calling for his death. Let's pray for those who are accused wrongly of a crime.

- Lent is almost over! If your Lenten sacrifices have slipped a bit, it's not too late to renew them.

Deep Dive

- *Hosanna* is a Hebrew word that means "Rescue us!" but is also used as an expression of praise.

April 11—The Atonement

He himself bore our sins in his body on the cross, so that we might die to sin and live for righteousness.
(1 Peter 2:24)

Just yesterday at Mass, we heard of the unimaginable sufferings that Jesus had to go through during his Passion and death. Yes, we know that God sent his son to us for our salvation, but we all have to face this question sooner or later: Why did Jesus have to die?

We use the word "atonement" to talk about what Jesus did for us on the cross. At the beginning of that word, we see two words squished together: "at one." Jesus came to make us one with God again, but first he had to undo the damage done by Adam and Eve. Through their disobedience in the Garden of Eden, the human race had taken on a debt that we couldn't pay. God wanted to show us his mercy, but his perfect justice demanded that someone bear the cost of sin. But what man or woman could make that perfect act of obedience to reverse the disobedience of our first parents? We needed help.

And so, Jesus, the New Adam, came, he who was fully man yet fully God. He who was like us in all things but sin. Only he could make a perfect offering to the Father on the cross. He bore the weight of our sins and accepted the death that we deserved so that we might be reconciled again with God. Through his death, we gained life eternal.

Ora et Labora

- We have no way to fully repay the great gift our Lord showed us on the cross. Let our prayer today be one of gratitude for our many blessings.

- Some people, like firefighters, put their lives on the line every day to save others. Talk with your parents about small ways that we can lay our lives down for others.

Deep Dive

- The word "redemption" comes from the Latin word *redimere*, "to buy back." Jesus Christ paid the price for our sins so that we could be redeemed.

April 12—Passover

The blood will be a sign for you on the houses where you are,
and when I see the blood, I will pass over you.
(Exodus 12:13)

The night before he died, Jesus and his disciples shared a special meal together called the Passover. Though it sounds a little bit like a football play, the Passover had nothing to do with sports. It involved blood and death.

You may remember the ten plagues that God sent down on the Egyptians when Pharaoh refused to give the Hebrews their freedom. Locusts, frogs, rivers turning to blood...it was all pretty awful, but Pharaoh's heart was hard. He did not want to lose his slaves. And so, the final plague was the worst: the death of all the firstborn children of the families of Egypt. God would send his angel of death that night, but the houses of the Jews would be "passed over" as long as they did the following: sacrifice a lamb without blemish, spread its blood above the doorposts of their homes, and then eat the meat of the lamb. The Hebrews did all that that very evening, and their firstborn children were spared. The next day, Pharaoh, who had lost his oldest child in the night, granted them their freedom.

When Jesus shared the Passover meal with his friends, he gave this old feast a new meaning. His disciples realized a few important things: Jesus himself was the spotless lamb of God that they were now to feast on in the Eucharist. They would also drink of his blood, which he gave to save us from death. And as the Jews were commanded to celebrate the feast of Passover each year to celebrate their liberation from slavery, we are called each year to celebrate the mysteries of our own deliverance from sin and death.

Ora et Labora

- Our Jewish brethren still celebrate Passover, which usually falls very close to our Holy Week. Let's pray for our Jewish brothers and sisters as they commemorate that holy night.

- When you have meals with your family, be grateful, respectful, and helpful!

Deep Dive

- Christians often talk about Jesus's Passion, Death, Resurrection, and Glorification as the "Paschal Mystery," which derives from the Hebrew word for "pass over," *pesach.* (PEH-sahk)

April 13—Spy Wednesday

Even my close friend, someone I trusted, one who shared my bread, has turned against me.
(Psalm 41:9)

Have you ever had a good friend let you down? Maybe you found out that someone you trusted was talking behind your back or just stopped speaking to you altogether. It's a hard thing to be treated that way by anyone, and especially by a friend.

This day is traditionally known as Spy Wednesday, because this is the day that Judas went to the High Priest to betray Jesus for 30 pieces of silver. We know how that turned out. He led soldiers to the garden of Gethsemane the next evening, kissed Jesus on the cheek so they would know which one he was, and then Jesus was arrested. Judas later felt so guilty over what he had done that he took his own life.

The question many of us have is why would Judas do this to his friend whom he had followed and trusted for three years? The Bible tells us that he was a greedy man, so maybe he did it for the money. Maybe he expected Jesus to be a different type of Messiah than he was. Whatever the reason, it's good to remember this: we are more like Judas than we think. We, too, mess up through our sin and let Jesus down. But we can make sure not to repeat Judas's gravest mistake: he felt that he was beyond forgiveness. Instead of turning to despair over our mistakes, we can turn back to Jesus and ask for his mercy.

Ora et Labora

- Let's pray for those who are in despair at this difficult time and would consider taking their own life.

- Forgiving others is so difficult. It can be just as difficult to forgive ourselves. If there is someone you're struggling to forgive, maybe now is the time. Remember, our Lord forgave those who had sent him to the cross even as he struggled for his last breaths.

Deep dive

- Traditionally a service takes place on this night called *Tenebrae* (TEH-neh-bray), a Latin word that means "darkness." As readings and psalms are prayed, candles are extinguished one-by-one until only one remains, which symbolizes Christ, the lone light in the darkness.

April 14—Holy Thursday

Jesus knew that the hour had come for him to leave this world and go to the Father. Having loved his own who were in the world, he loved them to the end.
(John 13:1)

The shortest season of the church year begins this evening: the Easter Triduum, the great "Three Days." In these three days, we experience our Lord's suffering, death, and resurrection. But first he shared one last meal with his beloved friends.

On this night, Jesus and his disciples gathered in the upper room to celebrate the Passover meal. Here, Jesus showed us a beautiful act of service when he stooped down to wash the feet of his disciples. For men in a dusty region who wore sandals all the time, you can imagine how filthy their feet were! He who had created the world now humbled himself and became a servant. Jesus told his disciples that they must do the same for others.

They shared the meal together and after they had eaten, Jesus lifted up the bread and said, "This is my Body, given for you," then the wine, saying, "This is my blood, poured out for you." And again, Jesus told his disciples that they were to do the same: "Do this in memory of me." This was the first Mass!

On this holy night, Jesus showed his disciples a great act of love and then gave them his very body and blood. They did not know at the time that tomorrow he would show them the ultimate act of love, offering his body and blood on the cross for all mankind.

Ora et Labora

- This is a special day for our priests, since the Church considers this the anniversary of when Jesus instituted the priesthood. Let's pray for our priests and for more vocations to the priesthood.

- Talk with your family about ways to make this a very special Triduum in your home. Service, sacrifice, and eventually, celebration are good words to get you started!

Deep Dive

- Usually on Holy Thursday morning, all priests of a diocese gather with their bishop at the cathedral to celebrate the Chrism Mass. At this Mass, the holy oils used in the various sacraments are blessed by the bishop and sent home with the priests to use in their churches.

April 15—Good Friday

For God so loved the world, that He gave His only begotten Son, that whoever believes in Him shall not perish, but have eternal life.
(John 3:16)

It seems weird to call this day "Good" Friday. On this day, Jesus was arrested while his disciples fled, he was falsely accused, whipped, beaten, crowned with thorns, forced to carry a heavy cross and finally, crucified. What exactly is so good about this day?

If you have a crucifix nearby, look at it. When the world sees this, they see a criminal who died in disgrace. But we see an act of love that destroyed death forever. Our sins no longer have a hold on us because Jesus paid the price with his blood.

On this day, the Old Testament prophecies were fulfilled. The righteous man has been condemned to a shameful death. The suffering servant has healed us by his wounds. The spotless lamb has been sacrificed to protect us from the angel of death. On this day, a new covenant between God and man has been made with the blood of Jesus. It is finished.

Ora et Labora

- There is a long-standing tradition of silence in the home between Noon and 3:00 PM, the hours that Jesus suffered on the cross before his death. Be mindful of how alone our Lord felt at that time, and let's pray for those who feel abandoned in our world.

- The Church asks us to fast on this day. This can be difficult, but drink a lot of water and when you get hungry, offer it up for those in need.

Deep Dive

- Many centuries ago the word "good" also meant "holy." And so, "Good Friday" means "Holy Friday."

April 16—Holy Saturday

"I am He who lives, and was dead, and behold, I am alive forevermore. Amen. And I have the keys of Hades and of Death."
(Revelation 1:18)

The day after he died, the earth was quiet as our Lord lay in the tomb. Well, he was also kicking down the doors of Hell like a superhero!

In the Apostle's Creed, we say that, after Jesus died, "he descended into Hell." Technically, he went to a special part of the underworld that we call "Abraham's bosom." The souls of the just ones were there, awaiting the day when the Lord would redeem them and lead them to their heavenly home. That day was today! These blessed men and women were the first to hear the good news of Christ's victory over the grave. The minions of Hell tried to stop Jesus's rescue mission into the underworld, but his saving death had made them powerless.

And so, as those on earth were mourning the death of Jesus, those below the earth were rejoicing as Jesus led their exodus from death's doorstep to the gates of Heaven. Tomorrow, all those on earth will receive the good news too, and we will respond with a great Alle—whoops, we can't say that quite yet! But soon!

Ora et Labora

- Thousands of men and women throughout the world have spent time in prayer and preparation and will enter the Catholic Church at the great Easter Vigil service this night. Let's pray for them as they will finally receive the grace of the sacraments.

- This is a day of "great silence because the king is asleep." Let's keep the screens to a minimum, and help your mom and dad around the house with whatever needs to be done to prepare for the great celebration tomorrow.

Deep Dive

- There is a beautiful Easter Proclamation sung at the Vigil service called the *Exsultet*. It is sung at the foot of the newly-blessed Easter candle while the church is lit only by candles held by the people. Probably the most well-known part of the prayer is this:

  O wonder of your humble care for us!
  O love, O charity beyond all telling, to ransom a slave you gave away your Son!
  O truly necessary sin of Adam, destroyed completely by the Death of Christ!
  O happy fault that earned so great, so glorious a Redeemer!

  (The text of the Exsultet can be found here: https://www.usccb.org/prayer-and-worship/liturgical-year-and-calendar/easter/easter-proclamation-exsultet)

April 17—Easter Sunday

O death, where is your sting? O grave, where is your victory?
(1 Corinthians 15:55)

This is the day! We celebrate Jesus's ultimate victory today...but he's nowhere to be found. The gospel reading from Mass this morning is unlike any other that is read during the year. Why? Because it doesn't have Jesus in it! Where the heck did he go?

This is how the faith of the early Christians began, in the reality that the tomb was empty. When the women came to anoint the body of Jesus, they found the stone rolled away and two angels that asked them,"Why do you look for the living among the dead? He is not here, but has risen." (cf. Luke 24:5-6) Can you imagine how they must have felt? Their greatest love was taken from them only days before. And now, they came and found that the grave had no hold on him.

Dear children, St. Paul tells us that if Christ had not risen, our faith would be in vain. (1 Corinthians 15:14) And here we are, faced with the empty tomb. So, let us rejoice this day. Christ is risen! Alleluia!

Ora et Labora

- Let your prayer overflow with joy this day! Sing your Alleluias loud and proud!

- Learn the traditional Easter greeting. One person says, "He is risen!" and the other responds with, "He is risen indeed!" Christians have been using this for centuries.

Deep Dive

- A special piece of music called a "sequence" is used at Mass today after the Second Reading. It's a fabulous poem that speaks of the great battle that took place between the forces of good and evil:

  Death and life fought bitterly
  For this wondrous victory;
  The Lord of life who died,
  reigns glorified.

  This sequence is called the Victimae Paschali Laudes; the text can be found here:
  http://cantusmundi.blogspot.com/2012/04/christians-praise-paschal-victim.html)

Sign up below for the Catholic Kid 365 email list. You'll receive reflections for the Easter season and beyond!
https://tinyurl.com/29jvmk9v

Made in the USA
Coppell, TX
25 February 2022

74076593R00056